BOSTON

BOSTON
A Pictorial History

St Botolph's from the Market Place, 1830s.

BOSTON
A Pictorial History

Neil Wright

Phillimore

1994

Published by
PHILLIMORE & CO. LTD.,
Shopwyke Manor Barn, Chichester, West Sussex

ISBN 0 85033 937 5

Printed and bound in Great Britain by
BIDDLES LTD.
Guildford, Surrey

List of Illustrations

Frontispiece: St Botolph's from the Market Place, 1830s.

1. St Nicholas' church, Skirbeck, *c*.1850
2. St Nicholas' church, *c*.1900
3. St Nicholas' church, post-1935
4. St Botolph's church, from Market Place, *c*.1900
5. St Botolph's church, from Witham, 1856
6. St Mary's chapel
7. Sedilia in St Mary's chapel
8. South porch, St Botolph's
9. Interior of St Botolph's, pre-1853
10. High altar of St Botolph's, pre-1853
11. Interior of St Botolph's, 1856
12. Gas lamp standard in St Botolph's
13. Gysor's Hall, South Square
14. Altar tomb of a knight, St Botolph's
15. First vicarage
16. Dominican friary, Spain Lane
17. Dominican friary, Arbor Club
18. St Mary's guildhall, South Square
19. Window in St Mary's guildhall
20. Shodfriars Hall, 1856
21. St George's guildhall, Pinfold Lane
22. Pescod Hall, 1856
23. Hussey Tower
24. Grammar School
25. Emigrants for Boston, Massachusetts
26. Market Place, from south, *c*.1900
27. Market Place, southern end, *c*.1750
28. Market Place, southern end, *c*.1810
29. John Fox's House
30. Old Butter Cross, Market Place
31. Butter Cross Assembly Rooms
32. New Assembly Rooms, 1822
33. *Old Three Tuns*, Market Place
34. Plan of Market Place, next to St Botolph's, 1776
35. The old Gaol and the *Ostrich*, Market Place
36. Market Place and St Botolph's, 1830s
37. 56 Market Place, *c*.1900
38. Bothamley's, 57/58 Market Place
39. Market Place, from the north, 1860s
40. Hunter's Tea Stores, 20 Market Place, *c*.1910
41. Market Place from south, 1842
42. Old house, Gully Mouth
43. Wormgate, from Stump
44. Wide Bargate, *c*.1900
45. Dolphin Lane
46. Town Bridge, pre-1802
47. Lincoln Lane area, from Stump
48. 20 and 20a Stanbow Lane, 1964
49. High Street south of Doughty Quay
50. *Royal Oak* and *Lord Nelson*, High Street
51. High Street junction with London Road
52. River Witham, above Grand Sluice
53. Grand Sluice
54. Warehouse at Grand Sluice
55. Haven between Grand Sluice and Stump, 1822
56. St Botolph's from river, 1790s
57. St Botolph's from river, 1798
58. Maud Foster Drain, near cemetery
59. Bargate Bridge
60. Seedsmen's huts, Market Place
61. Wide Bargate sheep market, 1840s
62. *Ram Hotel*, Wide Bargate
63. Donnison's Corner, Sleaford Road
64. Packhouse Quay and Stump, 1795
65. Packhouse Quay and Stump, *c*.1900
66. Packhouse Quay and warehouses, *c*.1900
67. London Warehouse, Packhouse Quay
68. South Square, warehouses
69. South Square, houses on east side
70. High Street, backing onto Haven
71. Doughty Quay, *c*.1914
72. South End, *c*.1795
73. South End, *c*.1900
74. South End, and ferry to Pulvertoft Lane
75. Garfit's Bank, High Street
76. Shipyards and south High Street, 1811 plan
77. Shipyards, 1852 plan
78. Fydell House, South Square
79. Memorial to Thomas Fydell
80. Duckfield Lane, off South Square

81. Wilford's Bank—banknote
82. Holden House, South Square
83. South Square warehouses, 1811 plan
84. Sheath's warehouse, South Square
85. Sheath's Bank—banknote
86. Building in South Square, possibly Sheath's Bank
87. Pishey Thompson (1784-1862)
88. Ingelow House, South Square
89. Ingelow's Bank—banknote
90. Ingelow House school, 1872 advertisement
91. Haven—to rear of Sheath's and Ingelow's properties
92. Premises owned by Barnards in Wormgate
93. Barnard's Bank—banknote
94. London Road, Skirbeck Quarter
95. Samuel Tunnard's premises, Wide Bargate
96. Wrangle's windmill, South End, 1798
97. Gallows Mills, 1795
98. Gallows Mills, c.1880
99. Hussey Hall, Skirbeck Road
100. *Peacock and Royal Hotel*, 1896
101. *Peacock and Royal Hotel*, advertisement, 1896
102. Good Intent windmill, 1796
103. Good Intent windmill, remains 1967
104. Town Bridge, 1802-7
105. Watch-house on Town Bridge
106. Bridge Foot, 1960s
107. Horncastle Road and Maud Foster windmill
108. Tuxford portable steam engine
109. John Oldrid's draper's shop, Strait Bargate
110. Extension to Oldrid's draper's shop
111. Lacey & Garratt, Strait Bargate
112. Kitwood's grocery and wine business, Strait Bargate
113. Cottages in Duckfield Lane, off South Square
114. Cottages in White Cross Lane, off South Square
115. Cottages in Smith's Yard, Wormgate
116. 23 Red Lion Street, Georgian doorway
117. Number Slabs, Witham Place
118. Pen Street
119. Liquorpond Street
120. Blue Street
121. Wall between High Street and Liquorpond Street
122. Witham Green
123. Seward's Passage, off Norfolk Place
124. Drainside South
125. South Terrace
126. Skirbeck Rectory, burnt down in 1847
127. Holy Trinity church, Skirbeck
128. General Baptist's chapel, High Street
129. Salem Baptist chapel, Liquorpond Street
130. Wesleyan Centenary chapel, Red Lion Street
131. Primitive Methodist chapel, West Street
132. Methodist New Connection, Zion chapel, West Street
133. Thomas Kitwood and Thomas Bailey, advertisements
134. Independent chapel, Grove Street
135. Jail, Poor House and National School, South End
136. Old Baths, 1852 plan
137. Bath Gardens Reservoir
138. Council chamber, Guildhall
139. Thomas Broughton's house, Wide Bargate
140. John Noble's premises, Market Place, 1842
141. Union Workhouse, Skirbeck Road
142. Grand Sluice railway bridge
143. Broadfield Lane locomotive depot—offices
144. Great Northern Railway granary
145. Passenger station
146. Railway goods sidings
147. Civil Engineeer's depot, Sleaford Road
148. Herbert Ingram (1811-60)
149. Duke Street
150. Queen Street
151. St James' church, George Street
152. *Lincolnshire Herald* and *Boston Gazette*, advertisements
153. Queuing for the *Lincolnshire Standard*, 1986
154. Boston Regatta, 2 August 1888
155. Post office, Market Place
156. Shodfriars Hall, 1873
157. Interior of Shodfriars Hall, 1873
158. Black Sluice area
159. Boston General Hospital
160. Boston Corporation baths
161. Basin of Boston Dock
162. Boston Dock—Workshops
163. Coal hoist on the Dock
164. Skirbeck Road
165. Forinton's furniture shop, later Wimpy Bar, West Street
166. Pupils of Boston Park Board School, 1899
167. Staniland Board School, Fydell Crescent
168. Boston Fire Brigade outside municipal buildings
169. General post office, Wide Bargate
170. Demolition of old Town Bridge, 1913
171. Erection of new Town Bridge, 1913

Illustration Acknowledgements

All of the pictures in this book are from originals or copies in the author's collection, and many are published for the first time. I would like to thank all the people who have given me pictures over the years or lent originals to be copied, in particular Mr. Clayton and Dr. M.J.T. Lewis who each gave me several about 20 years ago, and Mrs. Isabel Bailey and Mrs. Pat Pomeroy who have in recent years provided me with copies of several they have found. Others are copies of originals in Boston Library. Mrs. I. Bailey, 140; Boston Library (Lincolnshire County Council), 2, 10, 18, 21, 26, 34, 37, 38, 40, 58, 63, 67, 70, 71, 82, 88, 111, 155, 170; Mr. Clayton, 3, 65, 73, 91, 107, 137, 161, 164, 169; Dr. M.J.T. Lewis, 66, 74, 125.

I must also thank Andrew Crabtree and Noel Pulford of Boston Guildhall Museum who have given me access to their collections and have helped me to obtain copies of: 9, 36, 41, 51, 55-7, 60, 80, 81, 85, 87, 89, 93, 96, 97, 102, 104-6, 113, 154, 156-60, 166, 168, 171.

Some have been reproduced from old publications, notably Pishey Thompson's *History of Boston*, 1, 5, 6, 8, 11, 13-16, 20, 22, 23, 27-33, 35, 42, 46, 99, 127-30, 141; early numbers of the *Illustrated London News* when controlled by its Boston-born founder Herbert Ingram, 12, 108, 126, 142, 148, and the magazine *Boston Society* published 1899-1902, 24, 87, 98, 131, 132, 134.

Photographs of Boston in the 1960s and 1980s were taken by the author, and others have been purchased over the years.

Introduction

Lying between the Wash and the Lincolnshire fens is a crescent of higher land called the townlands, and where the river Witham cuts through this protective barrier is the town and port of Boston. Around Boston the wide open skies dominate the great flat fenland fields which stretch to meet at the distant horizon. Some parts of the fens are at or below sea level, but the townlands are 10 or 15 ft. higher. For 200 years the long straight lines of the canalised river Witham and several navigable drains have converged on the historic capital of this part of the fens. Despite being almost entirely man-made, the modern landscape of the fens still retains an atmosphere of solitude and mystery. In Roman times a semi-circle of islets curving round the Wash filled much of the Lincolnshire fenland, and they later coalesced as the townlands to form a barrier between the inland fens and the seaward marshes.

At the time of the Norman Conquest Boston was part of the parish of Skirbeck but it soon achieved a separate identity as the port for the city of Lincoln. Boston was developed by Alan Rufus, son-in-law of William the Conqueror, and was part of the extensive estates called the Honour of Richmond given to him in 1071. Alan's property in Boston was the Manor of Hallgarth which lay east of the river, whilst the west side belonged to the families of De Croun and De Tattershall. Here goods could be transferred from river craft to larger seagoing vessels, and vice versa. Until about 1400 the town was called St Botolphs, after the patron saint of its church, but even then its shorter modern name was coming into use. Its parish was formed out of Skirbeck which lay south and east of Boston in two parts separated by the river Witham which, through Boston and downstream of the town, is known as the haven. To the north and west were huge unenclosed fens: East, West, Wildmore and Holland.

In the Middle Ages the fens were a great tract of undrained flat land traversed by the windings of sluggish streams. In winter they were a mixture of marsh and bog and black stagnant pools, but in summer they became parched deserts as all except the deepest pools dried up. The fens might have seemed desolate and oppressive but common rights over them to graze sheep, cattle, horses and geese, dig out turf, gather reeds for thatch and fish the pools and watercourses were of value to the people of Boston and adjacent villages. The land appeared to be all of a level but folk steeped in the lore of the old fens knew where islands would appear when the spring or tidal floods arose, and identified them by names which have largely been forgotten for a century or more. Eighty years or so after the Conquest there was a religious revival in England, and the loneliness and desolation of the medieval fens attracted the Cistercian Order who founded monasteries near Boston at Swineshead, Kirkstead and Revesby. The monks came originally for solitude but in a short time they had established massive flocks of sheep and contributed greatly to the wealth of England.

Wool was the most important export of medieval England and went to Flanders, Italy and elsewhere. Lincolnshire, as one of the main wool-producing counties, enjoyed great prosperity and Boston as its main port became one of the busiest in the kingdom. The quays were the heart of Boston and were established along both banks of the river. Soon the town was trading in its own right and at its peak in the 13th century the value of the goods passing through the port, as measured by the customs dues, indicated that it was the second most important in England. The manor of Hallgarth was but one of many estates belonging to one of the great magnates of the kingdom and the manor house (east of the present grammar school library) fell into disrepair as the lord's officials conducted their business in the more central Gysor's Hall (built before 1248) in South Square.

Boston Fair, first mentioned in 1125, was where deals were done and it became one of the greatest fairs in Europe. Several prominent wool-producing monasteries in northern and midland England had houses here which were used during the fair. On fair-days booths were set up and English merchants and monks haggled with foreign merchants over exports of wool, salt and lead from England and imports of cloth from Flanders, wine from France and Italy, timber, steel, furs and falcons from the Baltic countries, leather from Spain, and spices and other luxury goods from the eastern Mediterranean. Buyers for royal and noble households came to Boston to purchase the best. From about 1260 the Hanseatic League of north European cities had a Steelyard or warehouse near the site of South Terrace. After 1300 Hanseatic merchants dominated the Baltic trade and in Boston they were active supporters of the friaries.

The main part of the town was in a strip along the east bank of the river, lying north and south of the parish church. It appears that the present grammar school yard was the original Mart Yard or market square, but the present Market Place was laid out either then or soon after near the parish church with burgage plots on its eastern side. The plots were end-on to the Market, and lanes between each pair gave access to the back of the plot; most of these lanes still survive, many with medieval names. Encircling this eastern half of the town was the Barditch, a moat which also served as an open sewer, and it connected with the Witham at each end.

As the town grew, houses were built outside the Barditch and the first such development was perhaps in Strait Bargate where the road leading towards Wainfleet and Spilsby crossed a bridge over the sewer. Strait Bargate led into Wide Bargate which until recent times, and probably from the earliest days, was the site of the town's livestock market. On both banks were roads running parallel to the river, with premises between them and the river itself for much of their length. On the east bank were Wormgate and South End (the latter now divided into South Street, South Square and South End) and on the west bank were High Street and Stanbow Lane. The west side of medieval Boston developed in a small area opposite the Market Place, around the point where the Town Bridge was built. The street names reflected that in 1272 many Lincoln merchants had stone houses in this part of the town, and the medieval street pattern remained until the 1960s when the area was redeveloped. The bridge may have been built as early as 1142, and its upkeep was paid for by toll charges levied by the lords of the manors on each bank.

The lord of the main manor did not live in Boston and there was no municipal corporation so the main embodiment of the corporate life of the town were the guilds, which were fraternities or clubs that performed religious, commercial and social functions. The leading officers of the guilds were effectively the main citizens of Boston, although the guilds included prominent people from outside the town, occasionally even royalty. Most guilds had a hall for their meetings and the wealthiest ones employed priests and owned expensive vestments, crosses and other sacred items, for use in processions and church services. There were about fourteen guilds in Boston and each of the main ones had a chapel in St Botolph's church. The guilds looked after their members in life and death, and some supported a grammar school in the town. St Mary's guild, founded about 1260, was the oldest and wealthiest and was associated with the wool merchants. Their guildhall, built c.1450, is now the Boston Museum. Next was the Corpus Christi guild which was founded about 1335 and had more than 100 members including bishops, abbots and peers from all over England.

The number of people with a religious vocation in medieval Boston was very great, and in addition to the priests attached to the parish church and the guilds there were also four friaries in the town and a few monks at St John's. The parish church was granted to the Benedictine abbey of St Mary at York in 1089 and it was under their patronage until 1478. The town prospered and in 1332 Boston was England's fourth wealthiest provincial town, with a population of five thousand. The old church was no longer adequate and in 1309 work started on building the present St Botolph's, which was completed by 1520. The building of this great church, which is still one of the largest in the country, reflected the medieval prosperity of Boston. As the stone church tower rose high above the town, the Stump, as it became known, could be easily seen from the distant hills of Lindsey and Kesteven and it became a guiding mark for travellers crossing the vast undivided common fens north and west of the town.

The great church reflected the wealth of medieval Boston, but even as it was being built the wool trade was in decline and with it the prosperity of Boston. The salt and wine trades were also going down for different reasons. At the same time the Fossdyke Canal and the river Witham were silting up, and trade from the Midlands looked to the Humber or even to the ports of southern England.

The Knights of St John arrived in Boston about 1230 and built a church and hospital for the poor and sick just south of the medieval town on the Skirbeck road. In 1482 they took over the patronage of the parish church and kept it until the Reformation when it eventually passed to the new Boston Corporation. The first friars in Boston were the Franciscans who arrived c.1260, soon followed by Dominicans, Carmelites (1293) and Augustinians about 1316-17. They each established a friary in the town, but after the Reformation the buildings were used as sources of stone and only parts of the Dominican friary now remain. There was frequent confrontation between the parochial clergy and the friars who were competing for the support of the people of the town and surrounding area.

The Knights of St John were expelled from England at the Reformation in 1540 and their Boston property, like that of the four friaries, later passed to the new Corporation. St John's church was derelict by 1500, following the Order's move to St Botolph's, and was largely demolished in 1583, although the churchyard was enlarged in 1715 and 1826 and continued as a burial ground for Boston until 1856. The hospital continued as the poor house for Boston until replaced by a new one close by in 1726, and in 1835 the Union Workhouse was built in the same area.

At the Reformation King Henry VIII got much property in Boston from various monasteries, friaries, the Order of St John and Lord Hussey (who had been executed for failing to put down the Lincolnshire Rising of 1536). The king gave this Boston property to his friend Charles Brandon, Duke of Suffolk, and the duke suggested to the leading townsmen that they should form a corporation and buy these land holdings and other privileges. In 1545 the king's illegitimate son Henry, Duke of Richmond, died and the

Honour, including the manor of Hallgarth, reverted to the crown and was also available for disposal. The leaders of Boston's guilds supported the scheme and part of the cost of obtaining the charter of incorporation was found by selling the gold and jewels of several of the smaller Boston guilds. The charter gave to the new corporation the manor of Hallgarth, the power to appoint the vicar of Boston, the right to send two burgesses to Parliament and all the other property which the king had in the town. The mayor and four aldermen were made the Justices of the Peace for the borough. The first mayor and 12 aldermen chose the 18 common councillors, and for nearly 300 years the Corporation continued as a self-appointing oligarchy. A number of leading members of the main Boston guilds were chosen as aldermen or common councillors of the new borough, including John Taverner, who was a leading composer of the day and master of the choir maintained by St Mary's guild in the chancel of the parish church.

The Corporation started business on 1 June 1545 when John Robinson (or Robertson) was sworn in as first mayor, the aldermen took office and a recorder and a town clerk were appointed. The leaders of the five incorporated guilds then handed over the deeds and inventories of their possessions, on condition that the corporation would continue to employ the guilds' 18 priests and 15 clerks and carry on their services, charities and obits. The ornamental plate and jewels of these guilds was sold and made a further contribution to the bill of £1,646 15s. 4d. for the charter. After the death of Henry VIII in 1547 the government introduced a stricter Protestant regime and Boston Corporation lost its former guild possessions to the crown and had to stop the religious observances. Lord Clinton was granted the property of the former Corpus Christi guild and the Earl of Northampton received the rest of the Boston property, returning St Mary's guildhall and other items to the Corporation who subsequently sold some of them. The Guildhall was used as the town hall until the 19th century. When the Catholic Queen Mary came to the throne the remaining Boston property still held by Lord Northampton (about a quarter of the original total) was taken from him and given to the Corporation in 1555. It was to pay for the maintenance of the Town Bridge, a grammar school and other uses; these were held as a charitable trust later known as the 'erection lands'.

By the time Boston Corporation was formed the town had already passed its medieval heyday and, like the rest of Lincolnshire, was something of a backwater. The people of the fens have always possessed an independence of spirit, nurtured by the nature of the land and the absence of great landed estates, and this has been reflected in many aspects of Boston's history since the Reformation. During the Middle Ages religion had been at the heart of the civic organisations of the town, and after the Reformation the link between church and local state continued as until the 1830s the Corporation owned the right to appoint the vicars of St Botolph's and was responsible for the maintenance of the chancel of the parish church.

In the early 17th century the vicars appointed by the Corporation were puritan in character, seeking to purify the Church of England by eradicating certain pre-Reformation practices, which they considered unacceptable. The Rev. John Cotton and the Corporation gave each other mutual support and the puritan character of the town attracted prominent people of similar beliefs. When Archbishop Laud decided to attack nonconformity, Boston resisted strongly but eventually about 250 people, including the vicar, member of parliament, aldermen, recorder, grammar school master and many other leading citizens, decided to emigrate to the virgin lands of North America. In 1630 most sailed from Southampton, others following shortly, and in Massachusetts they founded a new town of Boston. The

Boston party included lawyers, administrators and clergymen and soon they had made the new Boston the leading town in British North America. One of the emigrants was Edmund Quincey of Fishtoft whose descendant John Quincey Adams became sixth president of the United States in 1825 and whose shortened name has recently been given to a new road in old Boston. A small group from the original Boston ran the Massachusetts Bay colony for nearly sixty years until King Charles II revoked their charter and imposed royal governors on them.

During the Civil War Boston was garrisoned for Parliament. Lincolnshire was between the Royalist north and the Parliamentarian east, but the nearest that Royalists came to the town was Winceby where they were defeated in battle in 1643. After the Restoration Boston continued in the doldrums for another 100 years or so but then entered the second most important period in its history.

The town's fortunes revived in the late 18th century as the surrounding fens were drained, enclosed and cultivated. The first major scheme was the embanking and straightening of the river Witham in the 1760s and the construction of the Grand Sluice at Boston. This reduced the risk of the fens being flooded either by high tides or by storm water from inland. It also allowed the division of Holland Fen's 22,000 acres between Boston and other adjacent parishes, and then their enclosure. The East, West and Wildmore Fens north of Boston covered 40,000 acres, and because of their size and many deep pools they would be very expensive to drain and reclaim. Only when the price of corn rose substantially during the Napoleonic wars did it seem likely that their enclosure would be profitable. That work lasted from 1801 to 1812, much of the cost being met by selling off vast areas in the heart of the fens which became the new townships of Eastville, Westville, Midville, Carrington and Thornton le Fen.

The reclaimed farmland became one of the richest and most fertile agricultural areas in Britain. Great long drains were dug, carrying the water into rivers that eventually made their way to the Wash, and they were wide enough for watercraft to carry the produce of the area into Boston. In dry summers water would be held back in the drains, and locks were provided to maintain navigation at those times. Vast areas were divided into new farms with rectangular fields separated by hawthorn hedges. There were few trees, except some to shelter the new farm houses and buildings, which were often on the banks of drains rather than next to roads.

Previously the sheep, cattle, horses and geese bred on the fens had been herded to London and other markets on their own feet, but after enclosure the fens were cultivated for cereals and other arable crops and the produce had to be sent to distant markets by road or boat. Boston was the nearest port to Holland Fen, and to the East, West and Wildmore Fens when they were later enclosed, and it expanded considerably to handle this trade. Granaries and warehouses were erected, wharves were built and then came shipyards and ropewalks. People with capital came to set up as merchants, young lawyers and doctors came to open new practices, and workers came for employment in the granaries, ships and subsidiary businesses which sprang up to serve the growing town.

Lincolnshire's rôle in the Industrial Revolution was mainly to supply food to the growing industrial areas, and Boston owed its prosperity to its key position in that traffic. Waggons and boats brought grain to the town by road and navigable drain, and most went out either inland along the Witham to the Midlands, Yorkshire and Lancashire or coastwise to London. While rivers were being made navigable and canals being constructed, the main roads of England were being improved by turnpike trusts, and those into Boston from the south-west were turnpiked in 1758. Tolls were collected from road users to pay for repair and upkeep, and the London Road tollgate at Boston was one of the busiest in Lincolnshire, the great amount of traffic on that road reflecting the importance of Boston.

Turnpike roads were generally better than other roads and their development allowed the introduction of regular stagecoach services from Boston to London in 1800 and later to other places. The elite Royal Mail started a service from London to Louth on 5 July 1807. The stagecoaches stopped at inns to change horses and refresh their passengers, and the coaching inns were important places in Georgian towns. On market days carriers' carts brought people to other inns from the surrounding villages. The waterways served a similar purpose, and market packet boats brought people from the new fen villages to landing places at the Grand Sluice, Black Sluice and Bargate Bridge. The Grand Sluice was built north of the town and a separate community known as Witham Town developed there. As well as a large inn, the *Barge*, there were also warehouses, a ropewalk, brewery, iron works, oil mill, later the gas works and several streets of poor houses for the workers in these enterprises.

During these late Georgian times merchants and brewers prospered and founded the first banks in Lincolnshire—Garfit's had been formed in 1754 but it expanded, and then came Gee's Bank in 1783 and later four others which prospered during the Napoleonic Wars. The six banks in Boston at the turn of the century reflected the town's commercial importance, because at this time most other towns had only one (or sometimes two). During the first half of the 19th century Boston was the largest town in Lincolnshire, its most active commercial centre and also had more industrial activity than any other town in the county at this time. Two of the first significant engineering works in Lincolnshire were established here by William Howden and the Radical William Tuxford. Other industries included the purification of feathers from the great flocks of fenland geese to produce pillows. As newcomers settled in Boston Methodism grew and flourished, and the long-established Baptists increased considerably while some other denominations also had enough adherents to open individual churches; later in Victorian times a few more Anglican churches were built.

The rising prosperity was reflected in town improvements. Commissioners were established with new powers to improve streets or build new ones, as well as to light the streets and employ night watchmen. Congestion in the town centre was relieved by two new streets—Bridge Street west of the river and New Street on the east. The Market Place was enlarged, a new theatre, swimming baths and new Assembly Rooms were built. Vauxhall Gardens were opened in 1815 as a commercially-operated recreation park on the edge of the town, and the free Bath Gardens were created in the 1830s on the river bank.

Boston was the boom town of Georgian Lincolnshire and attracted many to share in that wealth, either as entrepreneurs or as workers, but the old oligarchy kept control of the Corporation and this led to increasing dissatisfaction among the newcomers. One of the leading families in Georgian Boston were the Fydells, and even after the death of Thomas in 1812 his extended family, including nephews and the husbands of his nieces, continued to dominate the Corporation until a new reformed body was elected in 1835. In the 1830s the whole kingdom was in a state of agitation about the question of reform and in Boston the confrontation was more serious than anywhere else in Lincolnshire. The reactionary Corporation called upon the Government to send in troops to prevent disorder, and they were here for several months.

Boston's experience was just part of wider national agitation over the Reform Bill, and in the end the Bill was passed in 1832. A general election resulted in a reformed Parliament, which then reformed other institutions. The Municipal Corporations Act introduced democratic elections to local councils, though the vote was only granted to men of a certain wealth. In Boston this resulted in a complete rout for the old oligarchy—reformers took all the seats and symbolically sold all the gold and silver plate used at civic banquets. In later years some of the pieces have been purchased back or donated because of their historic interest.

During the late 18th century the newly-arrived workers were evidently accommodated in new houses on the existing streets laid out in the Middle Ages, or in courts and lanes leading off them. But by about 1800 when the reclamation of the northern fens presaged a further growth in population, new streets were laid out on the edges of the town and groups of houses were built by small developers. There were three main areas of new streets: to the north around Witham Place and Witham Green, east around Pen Street and Main Ridge, and west in the Liquorpond Street area. Expansion into Skirbeck started along the east bank of the Maud Foster Drain (which had been named after a woman who owned land in the area when the drain was cut in the 1560s) and in Spilsby Road. Other smaller developments included South Terrace and part of London Road in Skirbeck Quarter. St Mary's Catholic church was established in Horncastle Road in 1826 and some Irish settled in the nearby North Street.

When the Great Northern Railway arrived in 1848 it took away the trade of the port and Boston suffered redundancy and poverty, relieved somewhat by the employment which the railway itself provided, until the construction of the dock 30 years later led to a revival. In 1900 the GNR was the largest employer in the town, with nearly 900 employees working in the civil engineer's yard, locomotive depot, sacking store and creosoting works as well as the passenger station and goods department. The company even had its own gas works to produce gas for lighting its passenger carriages.

Between 1851 and 1881 the population of Boston remained virtually the same, and it was overtaken by Lincoln and Grimsby which were then launching into great growth. Nevertheless there were several new streets built on the edges of Boston, including some for railway workers close to the line on the western edge of the town. Merchants suffered from the decline of the port but shopkeepers still prospered, the feather industry expanded and other new businesses, such as oil mills and the manufacturing of labels and cigars, arose. Consequently there were some people in the town who could leave behind their poorer houses in the centre and move into healthier houses, with gardens to front and rear, on the edges of the town, particularly in the Sleaford Road and Carlton Road area near the railway station and the select area of Spilsby Road. In the 20th century the town continued to expand into Skirbeck and Skirbeck Quarter and in 1932 Boston took over the built up parts, with a circle of land beyond for future expansion. In 1974, under local government reorganisation, a new Borough Council added the rural parishes of the former Boston Rural District to the borough.

There were also civic improvements in the late 19th century, including the cemetery, People's Park, General Hospital, Corporation swimming baths and new municipal buildings. Many of these buildings, as well as the dock, were designed by the borough surveyor, William Henry Wheeler, whose own home is now part of the borough council offices on London Road.

With the proposals for the first railways there had been plans for the construction of a wet dock as ships were becoming too large to use the tidal port in the town centre. For over thirty years private enterprise failed in its efforts but finally Boston Corporation took the lead and the dock was opened in 1884. Trade increased and soon fishing fleets were established as well. The deep sea fishing fleet left Boston in 1927 but commercial traffic has continued to expand and the dock estate took over much land at the southern end of the town. The dock has recently been sold to a local company.

In the late 19th and early 20th centuries some new industries developed, including oil seed milling, pea-processing and food canning but these had all ceased by the late 20th century, as had some older industries such as cigar manufacturing, malting, brewing and brick making. One of the few old industries which has survived and developed has been feather-processing, which now also uses man-made materials in its bedding. There were formerly several firms in this industry but for most of the present century it has been concentrated in the firm of E. Fogarty & Co. The label manufacturing started by Fisher Clark & Co. in the mid-19th century also still flourishes, now as Norprint. The success of the dock has also been reflected in the growth of associated firms, particularly timber importers, and the decline in use of the railway has been matched by the growth of road haulage firms in the town.

The remains of the town's medieval history mostly lie beneath our feet awaiting investigation by archaeologists, but a handful of individual buildings do remain and most streets in the centre of the town still follow the medieval pattern. The endpapers at the front and back of the book are reduced copies of the large scale Ordnance Survey plans of the town in 1887, and most places referred to in this Introduction and the captions to the pictures can be found on those plans. Medieval remains include St Botolph's church and Blackfriars, both built of stone, the brick Guildhall and Hussey Tower and also timber-framed houses at 25 and 35 High Street and Pescod Hall. Many of the buildings in central Boston date from the great Georgian period of prosperity, while around it are late Georgian and Victorian streets with the houses of prosperous merchants and shopkeepers, and then a further circle of 20th-century estates. At the heart is the historic port, which still has some old granaries and warehouses in contrast to the later dock further south where virtually all historic buildings have been demolished. There are few medieval remains but the Georgian and Victorian story is well illustrated by surviving buildings and by prints and photographs.

1 Boston was originally part of Skirbeck, whose parish church of St Nicholas stands beside the bank of Witham Haven a mile below St Botolph's. This church suffered the loss of its chancel and shortening of the nave to form a new chancel as shown here before restoration began in 1869. Until the 19th century Skirbeck was an agricultural parish with few inhabitants.

2 The Early-English church of St Nicholas has been extensively restored, though the distinctive circular windows of the clerestory are original. The church was restored, enlarged, re-roofed and refitted in 1869-75 to the condition shown here by the architect Sir George Gilbert Scott, whose father-in-law was John Oldrid of Boston. The tower was restored in 1899 when the present west window was inserted.

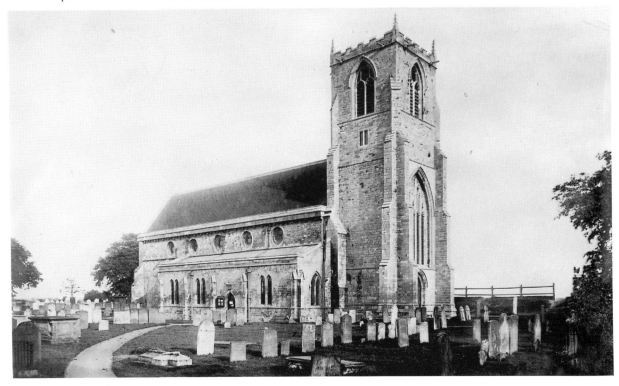

3   Since 1800 Boston's suburbs had spread into Skirbeck and they were absorbed into the borough in 1932. Soon after, in 1933-35, St Nicholas' church was extended by the erection of the chancel designed by L.T. Moore. As Sir George Gilbert Scott faced the external walls with new stone in 1869-75 and the tower was restored in 1899 the whole church looks surprisingly new.

4 St Botolph's, one of England's largest parish churches, was built around its smaller Norman predecessor. The foundation stone was laid in 1309 at the western end but then work started on the chancel and moved westwards along the nave and aisles. By *c*.1390 it was complete except for the tower and the addition of two eastern bays to the chancel.

5 The Stump or church tower at 272 ft. high is the most massive parochial steeple in England and reflects the medieval wealth and prestige of Boston thanks to the wool trade. Construction of the tower began *c*.1425-30 and it had two additional stages added before it was completed *c*.1510-20, when Boston was well past its medieval peak.

6 The chapel of St Mary's guild, the oldest and richest guild in Boston, was originally at the eastern end of the south aisle of St Botolph's, shown here in 1856. Remains of doors at two levels indicate the site of a parclose screen separating the chapel in the two eastern bays from the rest of the church.

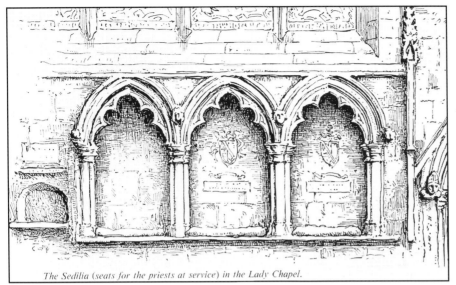

The Sedilia (seats for the priests at service) in the Lady Chapel.

7 In the former chapel of St Mary's guild is this aumbry to hold the sacred vessels for the mass and the three-bay sedilia or seats for the priests during service. The guild owned sacred relics and until the Reformation this was a place of pilgrimage. In 1545 the guilds surrendered their valuables and property to the new Boston Corporation.

8 The south porch is two-storey—Decorated below, Perpendicular above—and to the left is the founders' chapel, now called the Cotton chapel. Since *c*.1635 the upper storey has housed the chained library founded by the vicar, the Rev. Anthony Tuckney. The Archbishop of Canterbury, who was then visiting gave his approval to the founding of the library.

9 Looking west along the nave of St Botolph's between 1781 and 1851. The pulpit of 1612 faces a miniature classical façade, presumably indicating the seats of the mayor and corporation. The wrought-iron gate across the nave separated the area for worship from the large public space at the west end used for the distinctly worldly, and occasionally violent, electoral hustings.

10 The high altar in front of the Perpendicular east window included a copy, made by P. Mequinon, of a painting by Rubens in an Antwerp church. This Corinthian reredos was removed 1851-3 when the large east window by G.G. Place was inserted and the painting now hangs by the north door. The modern reredos by W.S. Weatherly was erected in 1890 and completed in 1914.

11 Looking east inside St Botolph's in 1856. The interior was drastically altered by G.G. Place of Nottingham in 1851-3, including the removal of the organ gallery across the chancel arch, insertion of a new east window, new font and pews. The ceiling, inserted in 1781, replaced 15th-century flat ceilings, but was in turn removed by Sir Charles Nicholson in 1928-33 from all except the chancel.

12 One detail of the 1851-3 restoration was the provision of new gas lighting by these distinctive standards, a number of which can be seen in illustrations 6 and 11.

13 The 13th-century Gysor's Hall belonging to the honour of Richmond stood in South Square and in *c.*1372 John of Gaunt, who then held the honour, made it the collecting point for the payments due to his manor at Boston. It was demolished in 1810 and some of its stones are incorporated in Haven Hall, the converted granary which now stands on this site.

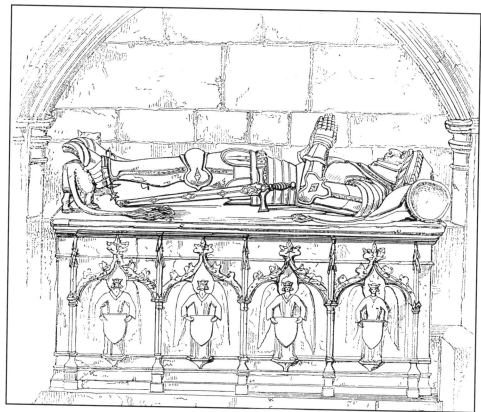

14 By 1281 the Knights of the Order of St John of Jerusalem had a church and hospital in Skirbeck Road. In 1482 the clergy moved to St Botolph's and their old church gradually decayed. Tradition says that this altar tomb of a knight, now in St Botolph's, was removed here from St John's church when that was finally demolished in 1626.

15 This building north of St Botolph's was the first vicarage built by the Order of St John in the 1480s. It was demolished in 1850 and its site is covered by a northern extension to the 1860 vicarage. The second vicarage (1751-1860) was in front of it, and the third one, now solicitors' offices, was on a site between the two.

16 This shows the main surviving part of the Dominican friary, now Blackfriars Arts Centre. Between *c.*1268 and 1316-17 four friaries were established in Boston as part of a religious revival. They were an important part of the religious life of the town until the 1530s after which their buildings were used as sources of stone for other buildings.

17 Other remains of the Dominican friary, which lay between Shodfriars Lane and Spain Lane, are in the ground floor of the Arbor Club in South Street. They include these three arches in the south wall, with infills, as well as a door in the north wall and a sculpture re-erected on the top of the front gable (rebuilt 1820).

18 In the centre of this picture of South Street is the hall of the guild of St Mary, built *c*.1450. The guild was formed in 1260 and was the wealthiest until, like the other Boston guilds, it handed over its assets to the new Corporation in 1545. Its hall was used as the town hall until the 19th century.

19 The west window of the guildhall, shown here, includes the few fragments of stained glass which survive from medieval Boston. St Mary's guild, like the others in Boston, served religious, charitable and social functions. It employed chaplains to pray for past and present members, and owned sacred relics and other vestments and religious items for services and religious processions.

20 This building, much altered in the 1870s, still stands in South Street between Sibsey Lane (*left*) and Shodfriars Lane (*right*). Called Shodfriars Hall since 1874, it has recently been suggested that it was the hall of the guild of Corpus Christi founded in 1335 by Gilbert Alilaunde and others. Until 1545 the guild's members included higher clergy, nobility and even royalty.

21 The guild of St George, founded in the 14th century, had its hall on the west side of the river, between Pinfold Lane and St George's Lane. On 12 July 1545 Boston Corporation took over the lands and possessions of the local guilds and St George's guildhall was used as a private house until its demolition in March 1898.

22 This picture published in 1856 shows the remains of Pescod Hall (*left*) viewed from Silver Street, with the buildings of Petticoat Lane between it and the Stump. The Pescod family were merchants in 14th-century Boston. The other building shown (*right*) bridged Mitre Lane (called Pescod Lane in 1581) so it might originally have been a gatehouse to the hall.

23 Hussey Tower off South End is all that remains of a mansion built *c*.1450-60 and later owned by Lord Hussey. He was executed for failing to suppress the Lincolnshire Rising of 1536 and his property seized by the crown and passed to Boston Corporation in 1545. The mansion was gradually demolished and since 1725 the tower has stood alone.

24 Some of the medieval guilds had supported a grammar school in Wormgate and that passed to the Corporation in 1545 but was seized by the crown two years later. It was returned in 1555 and in 1567 this building was erected in the Hallgarth. A porch was added in 1850 but it remained the only classroom until the 1890s.

25 By the early 17th century Boston was a centre of Puritanism and came under increasing pressure from authorities outside the town. In the 1630s many leading citizens left for North America and founded a new Boston in the wilderness. These men from old Boston ran Massachusetts, Britain's most prosperous colony on the mainland, for the next 50 years.

26 To the south and east of St Botolph's is the vast irregular shape of the medieval Market Place. Most of the buildings are Georgian, reflecting Boston's second great period of prosperity, though some façades hide older structures. The Georgians also opened up and enlarged it by demolishing freestanding buildings and blocks of property in the centre and on the west side.

27 These buildings stood in the south-west corner of the Market Place, and Bridge Street passed behind them on the left to give access to the Town Bridge. Those on both sides of Bridge Street were demolished *c*.1770 and the Corporation Buildings erected further back. The circle of stones on the left was the Fish Market which was included in the new building.

28 This block of buildings (*centre*) was demolished *c*.1812 and most of the site was added to the Market Place. To their right was Angel Lane (formerly Peacock Lane) and beyond that the *Angel* inn (now East Midlands Electricity showroom). The *Angel* was built *c*.1772 on the site of the 1611 assembly rooms, converted into three butcher's shops in 1748.

29 Down Angel Lane at its junction with Butcher Row (now called Church Street) stood the house where John Fox, who wrote the famous anti-Catholic *Book of Martyrs*, was born in 1515. In 1799 this was a public house called the *Bell* which later became the *Rum Puncheon*, now *Martha's*.

30 This cross stood in the middle of the Market Place, opposite Dolphin Lane, until taken down in 1730. The Butter Cross Assembly Rooms were then built on the site. Another market cross in South Square was referred to in 1564 and 1657 and the stalls where Joiners, Coopers, Basket-makers and others sold wooden wares were around that so-called White Cross.

31 The Butter Cross Assembly Rooms wer built by Boston Corporation between 1730- with a market for the sale of butter, cheese etc. and a room above for public meetings dances and other social events. The turret clock and sundial were added in 1745. It wa demolished in 1822 when the presen Assembly Rooms were opened next to th Town Bridge.

32 The final stage in the Georgian redevelopment of the Market Place was the opening of the present Assembly Rooms on 1 April 1822. Fish merchants still occupy part of the ground floor as they have done for nearly two centuries. Its southern end (*left*) extended over the approach to the old Town Bridge, which had been replaced by one alongside in 1802-7.

33 Despite the surroundings shown in this drawing, this building was actually in the Market Place until *c*.1820, at the south-east corner with Church Lane. It is alleged that Oliver Cromwell stayed here before the Battle of Winceby (1643), and by 1799 it was the *Old Three Tuns* public house. Its site is now covered by the last two shops at the end of the crescent.

34 This plan drawn in 1776 and copied in 1807 shows some of the buildings cleared away for the enlargement of the Market Place and the churchyard, including the Butchery and stocks (*centre*), gaol, *Ostrich* inn, and also the *Old Three Tuns*. Item M is the little shop of John Harrison to whom William Brand, the artist, was apprenticed for seven years (*see* no.35).

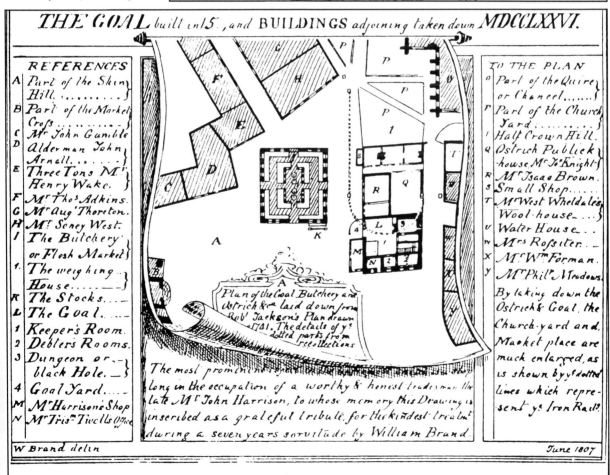

SKETCH OF THE GAOL, BUTCHERY and OSTRICH INN,
WITH SURROUNDINGS,
From Robert Jackson's Plan drawn in 1741, and re-drawn by William Brand in June, 1807.

35 The *Ostrich* [Oster-reich = Austria] inn occupied most of the western end (*left*) of this building, and the gabled section (*right*) was the borough gaol from *c*.1572. After demolition in 1776 the site was divided between the Market Place and the churchyard; iron railings between stone piers were erected along the new boundary. Left is the Butchery with stocks in front.

36 This print of the 1830s shows the view of St Botolph's from the Market Place after the removal of the gaol and butchery. Notice the small panes of the shop windows; between the 1840s and the 1860s (*see* no.39) plate glass became almost universal. From 1822 until the 1870s the Butter Cross clock was on Cave's Building beside the church.

37 This corner building in the Market Place was occupied as a grocer's by Sarah Magnus from the 1820s to 1840s, and she was succeeded by Thomas Small. From *c*.1860 to the 1980s it was a gentlemen's outfitters belonging to John Chambers and a succession of other firms. By 1935 it was united with no.55 and they were rebuilt in the mid-20th century.

BOTHAMLEY,
Best and Cheapest House for Watches, Clocks, Jewellery, and Wedding Rings. Agent for Henry Lawrence's Spectacles,
57 & 58, MARKET PLACE, BOSTON. ESTABLISHED 1795.

38 No.57/58 is a mid-17th-century building which still contains some re-used 17th-century panelling and doors on the second floor and 18th-century panelling on the first floor. From pre-1826 to post-1922 it was occupied by the Bothamley family, silversmiths, and for 50 years after *c*.1930 it was Dowlman's Bakers who were the last traders in the Market Place to live above the shop.

39 (*above left*) This 1860s view looking south along the Market Place was published by James M. Newcombe of no.12 (*left*). A number of such Victorian 'skyscrapers' were erected on narrow medieval plots along the east side of the street, towering over their neighbours. On the right Georgian symmetry predominates, including a crescent of six identical shops.

40 (*right*) On 26 August 1898 Pearks Stores opened a grocery at 20 Market Place, but 'Hunters Tea Stores' had it from pre-1909 to post-1955. It was run by Halfords in the 1960s as a cycle shop and since 1990 it has been part of the Superdrug shop.

41 (*above right*) This picture of 1842 looks north across the Market Place soon after it assumed its modern shape. The *Peacock* (*right*) was the main inn used by stagecoaches until the railway killed them in 1848. The inn, latterly the *Peacock and Royal*, was closed in 1965 and a new Boots chemist opened in 1967.

42 The Gully Mouth was originally a creek but it is now a culvert or sewer entering the river south of the present Town Bridge. Until 1750 this old house belonging to the corporation stood north of the Gully Mouth and it was evidently replaced by the one shown in no.46 between the old bridge and the Corporation Building.

43 This 1963 view of Wormgate, looking north from the Stump, shows the street curving to follow the former bend of the river. In the Middle Ages a number of priories and abbeys had property here and the guild's grammar school was in the bottom left corner of the picture. Bottom right is the Church House.

44 This surprisingly empty view of *c.*1900 shows the western end of Wide Bargate with Strait Bargate (*centre*) beyond. Livestock markets were held in Wide Bargate from the Middle Ages until *c.*1970. Permanent iron railings and pens were erected in 1871 to replace the old wooden ones brought out for each market day.

45 The main access to the fields east of the town centre between the Barditch and the Maud Foster Drain was via Dolphin Lane to the green lane cul-de-sac called Main Ridge. By the 18th century a footpath continued eastwards to a footbridge over the drain. Dolphin Lane still includes the old building (no.6-8) shown here.

46 Until 1807 the Town Bridge was just north of the present one, and was rebuilt four times after the 13th century—in 1358, 1557, 1631 and 1742. The pier built in 1500 as part of a sluice remained until 1818. Lords of manors, and then the Corporation, charged tolls on bridge users until the 1830s (*see* no.170).

47 Stanbow Lane (foreground) and Lincoln Lane (diagonally from left) formed the core of medieval Boston west of the river. The area was cleared in the 1950s to '70s and then redeveloped, and this picture of 22 August 1964 from the Stump shows some buildings still remaining in lanes on the left. The building centre foreground was Boston's temporary cottage hospital between 1871-4.

48 This picture shows two shops in Stanbow Lane, on the corner with Pinfold Lane, in 1964. This area north-west of the Town Bridge was a network of narrow lanes and old buildings, many of great age like the one shown here, which were cleared by the 1970s and the site used for a supermarket, office building and police station.

49 West of the river the main street southwards was High Street (called Goat Street or Gowt Street until *c.*1800) which became London Road when it entered Skirbeck Quarter. This picture of 3 October 1964 shows buildings south of Doughty Quay being demolished to clear the way for the new Haven Bridge which crossed the river behind them.

50 The construction of Haven Bridge Road in the mid-1960s required the demolition of the *Lord Nelson* (*left*) and the *Royal Oak* on the west side of High Street. Other public houses in High Street also had maritime or naval connections, including the *Rodney and Hood* and the *Anchor*.

51 This view shows the point where High Street (*right*) becomes London Road (*left*). The parish boundary was the Old Hammond Beck which ended in a basin (see large tree left of centre). The outfall of a sluice under the road emerged in the middle of a mud bank; this sluice or gowt gave High Street its old name.

52 In the 1760s the river Witham was improved for drainage and navigation, and this view shows the new channel north of Boston. Extensive riverside fens between Lincoln and Boston were reclaimed, enclosed and planted with crops for the first time. The port flourished as cereals and other crops from these areas passed through it to London and elsewhere.

53 This print shows the Grand Sluice which was built 1764-6 in a green field north of Boston as part of the Witham improvements. The sluice kept out the tides, to reduce erosion, and held back the inland waters to facilitate navigation. The structure, including the bridge, still survives, though much altered. An inland port developed here just outside the town.

54 This late 18th-century warehouse was built by the Witham Navigation Commissioners next to the wharf at the Grand Sluice. The warehouse, divided into four units, was to meet the needs of shippers who stopped here instead of going through the lock, which was part of the sluice, into the harbour.

55 (*above left*) This print published 1 July 1822 shows the old bend between the Grand Sluice and the Stump. In 1826 this bend was removed, the river straightened, and the land next to Witham Place (*left*) reclaimed to form raised gardens. The Grand Sluice was built in a large field and until 1766 the river channel came in from the right.

56 (*right*) After the 1760s most boats coming down the river from Lincoln stopped at the wharf above the Grand Sluice. Nevertheless this late 18th-century print shows a number of small boats moored alongside the bank next to the churchyard. The Market Place is beyond the railings left of the church.

57 (*above right*) This print of 1798 still shows small boats moored alongside the churchyard or drawn up onto the bank, but this custom was finally ended in the 1840s as Victorians objected to goods being unloaded among the gravestones. By 1798 several elegant Georgian houses had been built in Paradise Row (*right*) and a screen of trees planted along the riverbank.

58 This view of *c.*1910 shows the Maud Foster Drain east of Boston, with the trees of Boston cemetery in the distance. Between 1801 and 1813 the huge East, West and Wildmore fens north of Boston were drained and reclaimed at great expense, and the scheme by John Rennie involved the widening of this drain.

59 The widening of Maud Foster Drain required the rebuilding of five bridges. The main one was Bargate Bridge, shown here, which carried the turnpike road from Boston to Spilsby. This site was also the terminus for market boats plying the navigable drains in the fens north of Boston, and next to the bridge was the *Queen's Head* pub (*right*).

60 Following the enclosure of the fens, Boston became one of the main corn markets in the kingdom. Merchants used small offices in Grants Lane and Still Lane and mobile huts in front of the *Peacock* inn brought out by horse each market day. These huts were later used by seed merchants until the 1960s.

61 This 1840s view of Wide Bargate shows the sheep market, one of the largest of its kind in England, in front of the large detached Georgian houses of prosperous merchants and professional men. Apart from Brough's carriage works (*right*) and Mill Hill (*left*) most buildings remain, though they and the newer houses in between are now shops and offices.

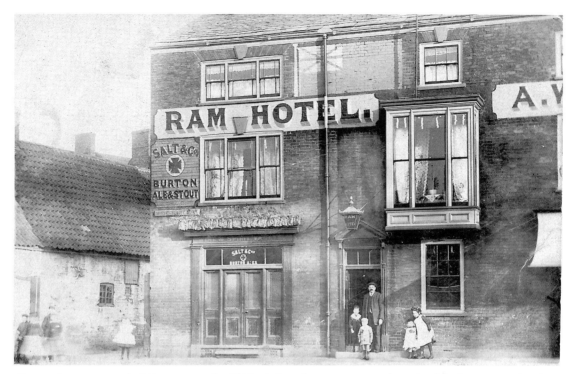

62 At the eastern end of Bargate, on the Skirbeck boundary, were a number of public houses catering for farmers and others attending the livestock markets. As well as the *Ram* there were the *Red Cow*, *Waggon and Horses*, *Queen's Head*, *Three Crowns*, *Cross Keys* (now called the *New England* hotel) and *North Pole* close to each other, but only three now remain.

63 This building was at the junction of Carlton Road and Sleaford Road and was removed earlier this century when a roundabout was built. It was called Donnison's Corner, and was on the site of the first toll-gate on the road to Donington which was subject to a turnpike trust from 1758 to 1877.

64 William Brand's drawing, published in 1795, shows Packhouse Quay which was the main landing place in the port, and the 1772 Corporation Building. Notice the steps leading directly from the harbour into the Fish Market beneath the centre of the Building, and the arch of the Gully Mouth at water level. The Fish Market later became the Police Court.

65 In 1814-5 a new river wall was built of brick and stone, removing the old projections and giving an even curve to Packhouse Quay and about one hundred yards northwards. The Assembly Rooms and warehouses extended out to this wall, and they somewhat overshadow the Corporation Building in this later 19th-century view. The borough council recently sold the Corporation Building.

66 This view shows Packhouse Quay on the right, with the tall Britannia Oil Mill (built 1850) behind, and on the far left a warehouse occupied in the early 19th century by Edward Wilford, who was a prominent merchant (*see* no.81). The left warehouse survives but the other buildings on the riverside have been demolished since 1946.

67 The London Warehouse, shown here, was built on Packhouse Quay by the Harbour Commissioners in 1817 following the improvement of the quay in 1814-5. This elegant building had classical proportions and a low pitched roof with long overhang. After the dock opened in the 1880s the river port declined and the warehouse was demolished *c*.1950.

68 After 1800 granaries came to dominate the western side of South Square, shown here in 1964 (*see* no.83). Four houses remain, including lawyer John Waite's (now the *Magnet Tavern*). Thomas Fydell built the far warehouse in place of Gysor's Hall in 1810, the next was built *c*.1810 by John Watson, and Abraham Sheath apparently built the right one *c*.1811-4.

69 This view shows South Square looking north. The late 17th-century house on the right was occupied by John Oldrid and family from 1833 to 1870, and then until 1916 by Mrs Dods, sister of Charles Rice, solicitor. Her father Charles Rice, senior, corn merchant, had built the house to the left *c*.1818 and the Rice family lived there until 1952.

70 This view shows the rear of properties on High Street, backing onto the harbour north of Doughty Quay. This is a jumble of roofs and outbuildings, with warehouses alongside public houses, shops and workshops. On the left, at the northern end of the quay, is the Public Warehouse with architectural details strikingly similar to the London Warehouse on Packhouse Quay.

71 This shows Doughty Quay in High Street, *c*.1914. This public landing place on the west side of the harbour also had a brick facing wall built 1814-5. In 1781 Henry Gee (1761-1845) arrived in Boston and in 1783 he and Henry Clarke opened the second bank in the town, with premises just off this picture to the left.

72 This picture shows South End *c*.1795, with a forest of ships' masts appearing above the granaries and warehouses in the centre of the port. The particular granaries were Clarke & Gee's on the left and Abraham Sheath's to the right of it. The house on the far right was where Pishey Thompson wrote part of his *History of Boston* in the 1850s.

73 This picture of *c*.1900 shows the size of vessels which could use the river. Left of the ship is the Buoy Yard used for the storage of navigational aids and in the foreground is the ferry between Pulvertoft Lane and Skirbeck Road. There was another ferry between London Road and the shipyards.

74 This *c*.1907 view of South End shows a number of wooden jetties along the riverside, which have since been replaced by a vertical river wall. On the left are late Victorian houses of Pulvertoft Lane. At low tide the ferry boat would stay in the middle of the channel with steps and planks down the mud on each side.

75 No.116 High Street, shown here, was the home of the Garfit family during the 18th and 19th centuries. William Garfit opened the first bank in Lincolnshire in 1754 and a century later they took over no.114 next door as 'Bank House'; in 1864 they moved to grand new premises at 51 Market Place now occupied by Lloyds Bank.

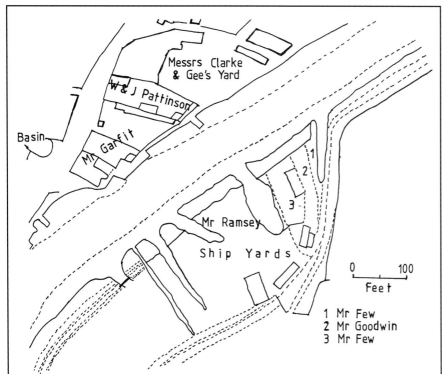

76 This plan shows the end of High Street (*left*) in 1811, where William Garfit and Messrs. Clarke & Gee each had riverside yards and warehouses. Mr. Gee was a banker, like Mr. Garfit. It also shows the Hammond Beck Basin (*see* no.51). On the opposite bank are shipyards on Corporation land called the Old Dock outside the flood protection embankment.

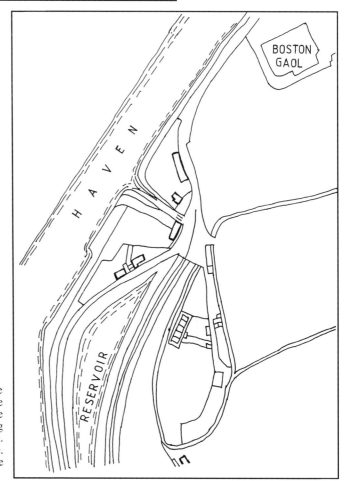

77 By 1852 John Richardson was renting all the shipyard at the Old Dock, including the house where he lived; Isaac Blackham, blacksmith, occupied the southern house. Only one creek remained, some having been covered by the 1832 embankment to the south. The Corporation Swimming Baths were later built here. The lozenge-shaped area to the south-east was the site of Wrangle's windmill (*see* no.96).

78 Fydell House in South Square was home to the merchant family who dominated Boston politics in the late Georgian period. They and their descendants owned it from 1726 until 1936 when it was acquired by the Boston Preservation Trust. After Thomas Fydell's widow died in 1813 it was occupied by their nephew Henry Rogers, the town clerk.

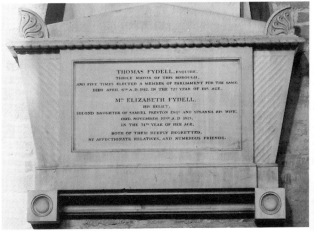

79 (*left*) South of Fydell House was one of the family's warehouses. This view in Duckfield Lane shows the south side of that warehouse, including part reduced to single-storey which still survives today. The 14 workers' cottages beyond it (*see* no. 113), where 50 people lived in 1841, were demolished between 1935 and 1955.

80 (*above right*) Thomas Fydell (1740-1812) is, like his father Richard (1710-80) and other relations, commemorated in St Botolph's. They were the leading family in Georgian Boston, though not unchallenged, and for twenty years after 1812 his extended family of nephews and nieces' husbands continued to wield great power in the town.

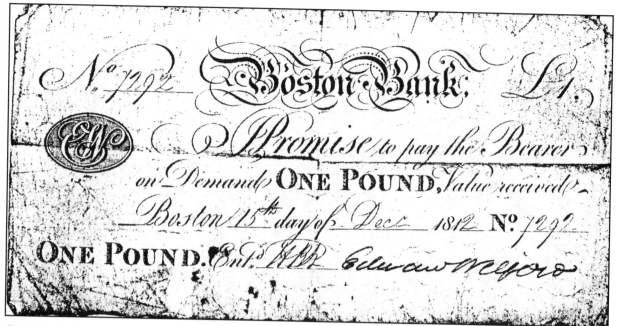

81 This bank note now in Boston Museum was issued in 1812 by Edward Wilford (b.1766), a prominent merchant and shipowner who at one time owned a dozen ships. He was a protégé of Thomas Fydell and married Thomas' niece Charlotte Rogers. However, like other private banks in Boston at the end of the Napoleonic wars, his bank collapsed on 13 January 1815.

82 This shows a house and granaries on a site which Abraham Sheath (*c.*1749-1816), another leading merchant and shipowner, owned by 1782. Sheath and his sons started a bank in 1789 but after it failed in 1814 this property was sold for £5,500. The house shown here was built after a fire in the 1820s when William Ingelow, Jnr lived here.

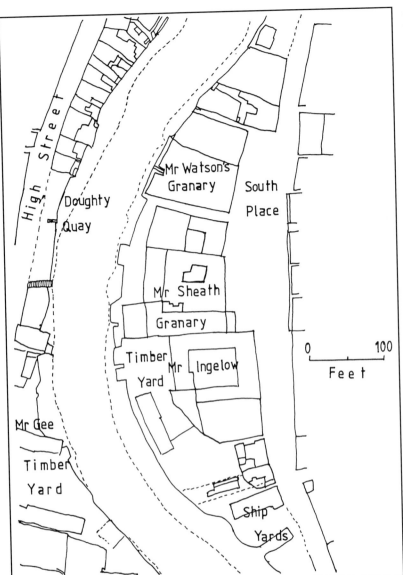

83 This plan of the harbour shows the western side of South Square in 1811. Mr. Sheath's house and granary were sold in 1815 and later rented to successive tenants including the father of Jean Ingelow the poetess. The house was replaced by the larger one shown in fig. 82 after the fire in the 1820s.

84 Sheath's property lay between South Square and the Haven. The original granary was south of the house, and later a wooden extension was added to the west. The tall block shown here between the house and the Square was apparently built after 1800 and remained until 1964 when the whole site was cleared.

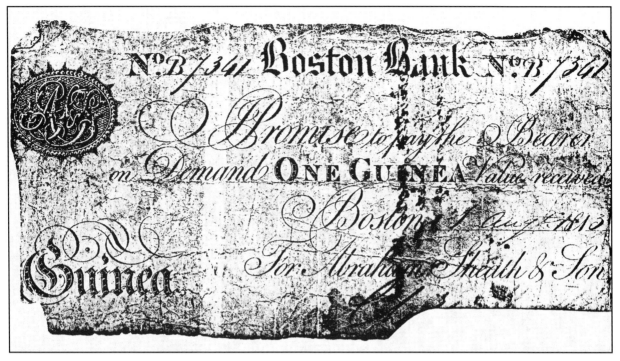

85 Sheath's Bank was in business for 25 years and Abraham established branches with other partners in Lincoln and elsewhere. This note issued in August 1813 was evidently signed by his son Challis. When Sheath's Bank failed on 29 June 1814, during the economic depression at the end of the Napoleonic wars, they apparently had notes worth £500,000 in circulation.

86 This picture of November 1964 shows the counting house projecting in front of the former Sheath granaries just before their demolition. Both the description in the 1815 conveyance and the architectural pretensions of the building suggest that this counting house was Sheath's banking premises. The arch, on the right, provided the only entrance to the rest of the site.

87 Pishey Thompson (1784-1862), the historian of Boston, pictured in 1859. He worked in Sheath's Bank until it closed in 1814, and then went to Garfits Bank as their First Clerk where he remained until he emigrated to the United States in 1818. He had an interesting career in Washington, including terms as Secretary of the Smithsonian Institution and as an advisor to the United States government, and returned to England late in life.

88 This shows Ingelow House, South Square, whose site is now covered by the eastern end of Haven Bridge. It was a square courtyard building with a mansion in front, granaries to the rear and a woodyard next to the Haven. The merchant William Ingelow, Snr (*c*.1765-1830) had founded a bank in High Street in 1805 and moved here in 1807.

89 Boston Museum has several banknotes issued by William Ingelow & Son, including this one issued in September 1825 and endorsed under their bankruptcy proceedings. Three Boston banks failed in 1814-5 but Ingelow's lasted until January 1826. Ingelow House was south of Sheath's premises, into which William, Jnr. moved after 1815 and where Jean, the poetess, was born in 1820.

INGELOW HOUSE,

SOUTH SQUARE, BOSTON.

MISS POCKLINGTON

RECEIVES a limited number of YOUNG LADIES, to whose religious and mental culture unremitting attention is devoted. It is the endeavour of the PRINCIPAL, assisted by Miss EVERITT, a resident Foreign Governess, and Professors of Eminence, to impart an accomplished and useful Education.

The course of Instruction comprises READING, WRITING, and ARITHMETIC (including the Mental branch), Plain and Ornamental NEEDLEWORK, ENGLISH GRAMMAR and COMPOSITION, GEOGRAPHY and the GLOBES, ANCIENT and MODERN HISTORY, ASTRONOMY, NATURAL PHILOSOPHY, the FRENCH and GERMAN LANGUAGES, MUSIC, SINGING, DRAWING, DANCING, &c.

TERMS, for Board, including the usual branches of an English Education, with French or Music, THIRTY GUINEAS per Annum. French, German, Music, Singing, Drawing, Dancing, &c., on the usual terms.

A Quarter's Notice, or a Quarter's Payment required previously to the Removal of a Pupil.

90 This advertisement was placed in the 1872 *County Directory* by Miss Francis S. Pocklington who after 1868 took part of Ingelow House and in 1871 had 12 resident pupils. The school soon passed to Misses Ann and Mary Adams, who took over the whole house, and later to Miss Cecily Matthews and then Miss Evelyn Rysdale until after 1919.

91 The paddle steamer *Boston* goes upstream passing, right to left, the Buoy Yard building, the rear of Ingelow House, and the former Sheath granary with its timber extension. On the far left is Doughty Quay. *Boston* and *Privateer* were paddle steamers mainly used to tow sailing ships along the channel into Boston from the Wash.

92 This building in Wormgate was owned by the Barnard family in Georgian times and the large arch gave access to a riverside wharf. The family were brewers and owned many public houses. They were also merchants who opened a bank in the 1790s. Unfortunately on 27 June 1814 they became the first bank in Boston to fail.

93 Samuel Barnard (1752-1810) from Norwich founded the bank, and was later recognised as the first active Radical in Boston politics. This note issued in 1812 is in the name of four of his sons—William, Robert, Thomas Lawrence and John James. Three of them lived in Skirbeck Quarter, where they owned much riverside property, so their bank was perhaps based there.

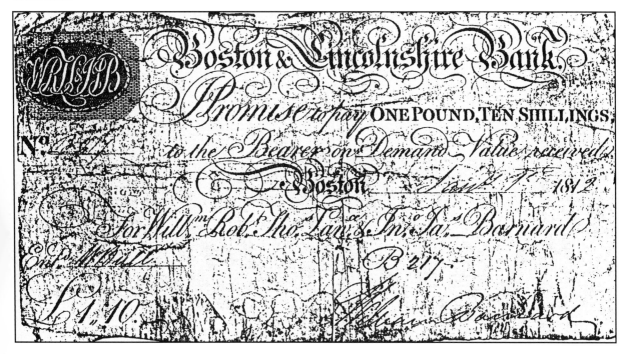

94 A continuous quay has now replaced the numerous jetties which used to line the Haven next to London Road in Skirbeck Quarter, in front of merchants' premises and old inns. The *Crown and Anchor* (second from the left), and the *Black Bull*, to its right, have both long closed but the *Ship* still remains.

95 This shows two of the large Georgian houses built in Wide Bargate in the late 18th century. The one on the left, now the Trustee Savings Bank, was built by Samuel Tunnard (1750-1818) of Frampton who set up as a lawyer and built the two-storey office next door after 1791.

96 In the early 19th century Boston and Skirbeck had about a dozen windmills. This 1798 view from London Road shows Wrangle's Mill in the foreground and the Gallows Mills beyond. Wrangle's Mill was on a mound about 200 yards south of the later General Hospital and was finally removed about 1825 (*see* no.77). The mound survived until the 1970s.

97 This view of the Gallows Mills was drawn by William Brand on 21 June 1795. The mills stood on the bank of the Haven at the southern end of Boston, just west of Maud Foster Sluice and St Nicholas' church. John Bailey became owner and occupier of the tower mill (*right*) c.1860, and in the 1870s also acquired the post mill on the left.

98 This photograph of *c*.1880 shows more accurately the elevated position of the two Gallows Mills on the bank of the Haven. Since 1795 the tower mill had apparently been provided with a new ogee cap and a fantail to turn the sails into the wind. Both mills were demolished in 1882 when Boston Dock was developed.

99 Hussey Hall stood in Skirbeck Road, south-west of Hussey Tower, but little is known of its history. In 1773 part was rented to a sail-maker and in 1779 it was surveyed for a gaol, but part was demolished in 1780 and the remainder, used by Gee & Clarke as a sacking factory in the 1790s, was demolished *c*.1800.

100 The *Peacock* dated from the 1670s with a late 18th-century façade to which the landlord, Daniel Jackson, added two bay windows and a balcony in the early 19th century. It was one of the finest inns in this part of the country, and the *Royal* was added in the 1880s after a stay by the Duke of Edinburgh, a younger son of Queen Victoria.

101 This advertisement of 1896 indicates some of the other activities at the hotel; there was also a shoeing smith in the yard, to look after horses hooves. Since 1848 Jackson and then Clemow also operated the railway refreshment room at Boston station, and for a time ran an omnibus to meet each train. The *Peacock* closed in 1965 and Boots the chemist opened two years later.

The GOOD INTENT" built by M.ʳ George Palmer in 1793

This Sketch drawn on the spot, by W.Brand, July.30ᵗʰ 1796. distance from Boston 1¼ mile, near the Sleaford Road.

102 The Good Intent windmill built by George Palmer in 1793, drawn here in 1796, stood south of Sleaford Road in the part of Holland Fen awarded to Skirbeck Quarter in 1769. It was later owned by Charles Rice (*c.*1783-1843) of South Square, a merchant in corn and wool as well as owner of this mill (*see* no.69).

103 The tower of the Good Intent windmill survived until 1967 when this photograph shows it being demolished. It was at the end of an access behind the petrol station on the south side of Sleaford Road.

104 In 1802-7 this cast-iron bridge designed by John Rennie was built south of the old Town Bridge (*see* no.46), which was not demolished until the new one was opened on 2 May 1807. The pier of the old bridge was difficult to remove and was only finally cleared in 1818.

105 The new Town Bridge, like its predecessors, was subject to tolls and the structure included this watch-house at the south-east corner. The Corporation's right to charge tolls was challenged and a court decision in December 1830 ended them. The watch-house was also used by night watchmen, predecessors of the police, but was latterly a sales kiosk.

106 Nos.2/4 High Street at the Bridge Foot (*centre*) were probably erected *c*.1802 when the new bridge was built, and were demolished *c*.1970. No.2 was a draper's shop for most of its history, occupied by the Walker family from *c*.1881 to after 1935. Soon after 1882 the Walkers also took over no.4, previously a shop called the Civet Cat.

107 When these children played in Horncastle Road cars were still rare in Boston. On the far side of the drain is the Maud Foster windmill built by Isaac and Thomas Reckitt in 1818-19. In recent years it has been restored to working order and is the only surviving windmill in Boston.

108 Boston had two of the first engineering works in Lincolnshire. Tuxford's, shown here exhibiting a portable steam engine at the Royal Agricultural Show at Newcastle in 1864, was founded in 1826 by the Radical William Wedd Tuxford (1782-1871), and in 1801 William Howden (1774-1860) had founded the firm which built the first steam engine in the county in 1839.

109 This shows the original five-bay shop in Strait Bargate where John Oldrid (1778-1849) set up as a draper with Richard Hyde in 1804. He was a supporter of reform and in 1838 was third mayor of the reformed corporation. The business stayed in the Oldrid family until 1901, and since *c.*1917 has been owned and managed by the Isaacs family.

110 Oldrids extended into this two-storey building in two stages: no.17 *(left)* was occupied by 1872 and no.15 *(right)* by 1885. The three-storey building between this and Oldrid's original shop was a printers and stationers where Robert Roberts first published the *Boston Guardian* newspaper in 1854; by 1905 it was Wing & Son who by 1922 had moved out for Oldrids.

LACEY AND GARRATT, Drapers, Milliners, and House Furnishers, 19 and 21, Strait Bargate, Boston.—The business which Messrs. Lacey and Garratt acquired in August, 1901, from Messrs. Thorns and Company, dates from the middle of the 19th century and may therefore

be properly cited as a well established business. Upon changing hands the premises were re-modelled and extended and a new front put in. The manager for seven years subsequent to 1901 was Mr. H. Page, who came from Woodbridge in Suffolk, and who two years ago became a partner with Mr. W. Lacey, of Louth, and Mr. Richard Garratt, of Grantham, in which towns these gentlemen carry on similar establishments. Having a thorough mastery of the trade and a complete knowledge of local needs, Mr. Page has been able to show some very pleasant records of success here. There is always a good display at Strait Bargate, both in the windows and within the shop—which is a comfortable one in which to move about and inspect the latest things in millinery, blouses, skirts, etc. Staircases—the ascent of which offers no difficulty as is the case at times in places of this character —lead to the millinery, mantle and costume show-room, and, on the top floor, to a spacious furniture show-room. The carpet and lino and fancy linen warehouse occupies the shop on the ground floor. Messrs. Lacey and Garratt are sole agents for Boston for ladies' " Pebrane " waterproof coats, also for the celebrated " Woolaine," " Ewe La," and " Wulma," blouse material.

111 About 1840 James Thorns started a draper's business at no.19 Strait Bargate (right). It traded under that name until acquired by Lacey & Garratt of Louth and Grantham in 1901, even though it had been acquired by Thomas Small, a grocer in no. 21, between 1861-72 and the drapery expanded into both properties. No. 19 was later occupied by Woolworths until 1961 when both were demolished.

112 Strait Bargate is a narrow curving street between the Market Place and Wide Bargate, and during the 19th century most premises were draper's shops. No.3 (right of centre in this 1964 view) was a long-established drapery until 1850 when Robinson & Smith opened a grocery and wine business, which became Kitwoods from c.1882 until it was demolished in 1968.

113 The port of Boston flourished after the enclosure of the fens and many of the first seamen and other workers attracted to Boston lived in lanes in the town centre. Fields were still so close that some lanes had a rural aspect, and these cottages in Duckfield Lane were only about 100 ft. from South Square (*see* no.80).

114 Before 1806 Thomas Fydell built nine cottages in White Cross Lane, off South Square, on the site of three earlier cottages. In 1841 there were 21 people living in eight of these cottages. By 1968 three cottages had been demolished but the six shown here, photographed in 1964, were still occupied.

115 These cottages were in Smith's Yard which was entered by a narrow passage off 20 Wormgate, and in 1861 there were 17 people in four houses, with two then empty. Their pantile roofs suggest that they were built before 1800.

116 Georgian houses have clear, uncluttered appearances with doors and windows regularly placed, their only indulgence being the door and its surrounds. Even a modest house like 23 Red Lion Street had a tall door-case including a window to light the hall, a nicely detailed surround, and perhaps originally a pediment over the top.

117 This 1964 view shows the row of houses called the Number Slabs in Witham Place which were built, between the Grand Sluice and Wormgate, between 1795-9 by John Watson, a speculative builder. This street was on the river bank until 1826 and the reclaimed land to the left then became gardens belonging to the elegant houses (*see* no.55). Behind them were streets of smaller houses.

118 By 1800 Boston's population was growing fast and new areas of housing were laid out on the edge of the town. This view looks north along Pen Street, the most important of a block of new streets laid down between Wide Bargate and Main Ridge. Since 1964 the properties on the right have been demolished to make room for John Adams Way.

119 Liquorpond Street was built in south-west Boston after 1800 and named after the pond of an adjacent brewery. Samuel Barnard laid out the street, and Blue Street alongside, with plots for groups of houses. Many ship's captains lived here, particularly in the finer houses on the right side, and there were also two Baptist chapels (*see* no.129).

120 Samuel Barnard was a Radical and he named Blue Street after his party's colour. The five houses on the left, and five houses behind them in a court entered by the passage shown, were part of a block of 13 built between 1826 and 1829 for James Roberts, a tailor and draper of Boston.

121 This wall was still standing on 19 March 1966 but since then it has gone and the fields on both sides have been developed for commercial purposes. The wall separated a pasture or park facing the High Street home of Mr. Claypon, the banker, from the Lord Nelson field adjoining Blue Street and Liquorpond Street.

122 This view shows Witham Green, an area of Georgian streets built to house people working in the river port at the Grand Sluice. Other houses were built in the adjacent section of Tattershall Road and a few between that road and the river—the whole area was known as Witham Town.

123 This picture of 1964 shows Seward's Passage, an early 19th-century row of four cottages reached via a narrow passage next to no. 22 Norfolk Place. These houses were lived in until the early 1960s. Until the 20th century most working people lived in houses rented from private landlords, and courts like this were often nameless until they were named after their landlords in the 1860s.

124 One of the most desirable areas in early 19th-century Boston was the east bank of the Maud Foster Drain called rather accurately but inelegantly Drainside (now Windsor Bank). It was actually in Skirbeck, as much of the parish boundary followed the drain, and this view shows part of Albert Terrace where some houses still retain their original windows.

125 This fine crescent of genteel residences, named South Terrace, was the acceptable face of a block of property developed by Thomas Dickinson (1788-1845) between 1829 and *c.*1844. Behind them were 25 poorer houses and after 1870 Dickinson's heirs raised about £3,500 in numerous mortgages on the estate until the mortgagees forced its sale in 1901.

126 This picture from the *Illustrated London News* shows the destruction of Skirbeck Rectory on Sunday 17 January 1847. The Rector from 1834 to 1853 was the wealthy Rev. William Roy, DD, previously principal chaplain at Madras in India. During his time he not only rebuilt the Rectory but also contributed to a National school (1840) in Spilsby Road and the new Holy Trinity church (1848) close by.

127 Boston's suburbs spread into Skirbeck after 1810 but were far from St Nicholas' church. The National school built in Spilsby Road in 1840 was used on Sundays for divine service until Holy Trinity church (shown here) was opened nearby in July 1848. This was another Boston building by George Gilbert Scott, architect of the then new Union Workhouse (*see* no.141).

128 (*above left*) Georgian Boston's economic boom benefited the spiritual life of the town and nonconformist chapels flourished. The long-established General Baptist church, supported by several prosperous merchants, rebuilt their chapel in High Street and erected the one shown here in 1837, including galleries added in 1841 and 1853. In 1842 they built a schoolroom in the neglected area of Witham Green.

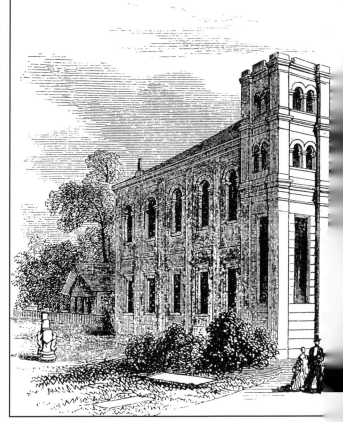

129 (*above right*) This view of *c*.1850 shows the Salem chapel in Liquorpond Street, a Particular Baptist chapel built in 1801 on land donated by Samuel Barnard, the developer of the street. A vestry and schoolroom were later added to the rear, but in the 20th century it closed and is now used for commercial purposes.

130 (*left*) There were very few Methodists in Boston until the early 19th century, but then the church grew quickly through the support of prospering newcomers to the town. A new chapel built in 1808 was replaced in 1839-40 by the larger Wesleyan Centenary chapel shown here. It was rebuilt after a fire in 1909 and still flourishes.

131 This was the Primitiv
Methodist chapel in West Stree
close to the station, in an are
where many railway worker
lived on the western edge of th
town. This chapel was built i
1898 and closed in 1965. I
replaced one built in 1865-
which burnt down in 1897, an
followed earlier buildings i
nearby Innocent Street an
George Street.

132 This photograph shows the Zion chapel in
West Street, built in 1829 by the breakaway
Methodist New Connection. The far end of the
chapel was destroyed by fire in 1859 but the
building continued in use until 1934 when the
congregation moved to the present Zion chapel in
Brothertoft Road. The old chapel became part of
the Regal cinema site.

133 Tom Bailey and Tom Kitwood not only shared one page in Kelly's 1872 *County Directory*, but also had their premises in the same street and were both leaders of Zion chapel in the mid-19th century (*see* no.112).

THOMAS KITWOOD,

BARGATE, BOSTON,

Wholesale & Family Grocer.

AGENT for W. & A. GILBEY'S

NOTED WINES & SPIRITS,

AND ALLSOP'S INDIA & PALE ALES.

AGENT FOR THE SOVEREIGN LIFE OFFICE & LANCASHIRE FIRE INSURANCE COMPANY.

☞ **THE ONLY HAT MANUFACTORY IN THE COUNTY,**

26, Strait, Bargate, BOSTON.

THOMAS H. BAILEY,

(LATE J. H. BAILEY & SON),

Wholesale & Retail Hat & Cap Warehouse.

A CHOICE SELECTION OF PARIS & FELT HATS ALWAYS IN STOCK.

SCHOOL CAPS, LIVERY & GENTLEMEN'S STANDARD SHAPE HATS,
MADE TO ORDER ON THE SHORTEST NOTICE.

SCARFS, TIES, SHIRTS, FRONTS, COLLARS, GLOVES, BRACES, HOSIERY, CARPET BAGS, GAITERS, &c.

THE TRADE LIBERALLY TREATED WITH.

134 Other new churches included the Independent chapel built in Grove Street in 1819. In 1841 a schoolroom was added to the rear. This photograph shows the chapel *c*.1900, but by 1965 it had closed and been put to other uses. Another Independent chapel was opened in Red Lion Street in 1850 and rebuilt in 1868 but that was demolished in 1974.

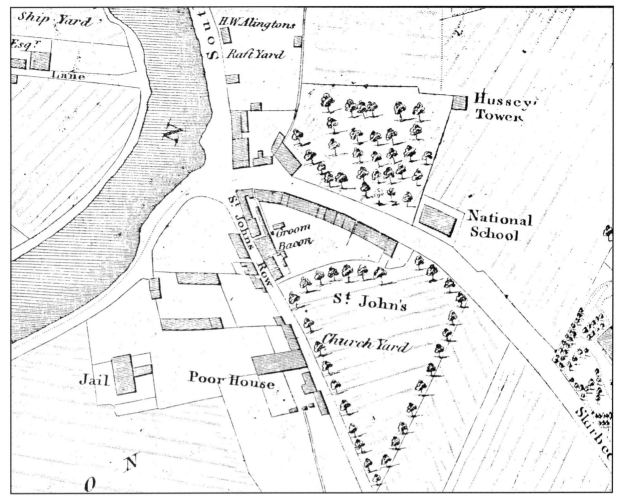

135 This 1829 plan of South End shows three important buildings of which no pictures are known. The parish Poor House was built 1726 to replace an earlier one nearby; it was demolished *c.*1837-8. The National school was built in Skirbeck Road in 1815 and in 1850 moved to Pump Square; the gaol was built in 1818, closed in 1851 and demolished in 1853.

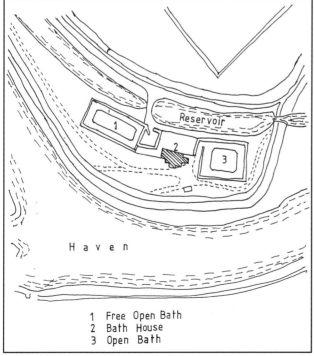

1 Free Open Bath
2 Bath House
3 Open Bath

136 Open-air sea-water swimming pools and a building for hot and tepid baths were opened in 1834 by a company assisted by public money. This plan of 1852 shows the original building in the gardens now covered by the Riverside quay of Boston Dock. The Corporation took over the baths in 1864 and built new ones nearby in 1879, closing the original baths (*see* no.160).

137 Here we see the northern end of the 1832 Bath Gardens, where much of the narrow strip between the new river bank (*left*) and the old bank (*right*) was filled by an elongated reservoir. In 1871 the Bath Gardens became part of the large People's Park then created on Corporation-owned fields behind the old bank. (*See* back endpaper.)

138 This view shows the council chamber in the Guildhall, used as the town hall until the mid-19th century. In the 1830s the oligarchy controlling the Corporation (including the friends and relations of the late Thomas Fydell) would not allow newcomers to join, and political tension in Boston rose to fever pitch during the reform agitation of that decade.

139 The house on the right, pictured in 1964 when it was part of the Lincolnshire River Authority's offices in Wide Bargate, was the home of Thomas Broughton who was mayor in 1828 and 1834. He was a brewer and tanner, with premises behind his house and in Pump Square, and leader of the Corporation's forlorn resistance to reform.

140 This billhead of 1842 shows the Market Place premises of John Noble (1788-1866), printer, stationer, bookseller and reporter for the *Stamford Mercury* (*see also* no.39). He was a self-made man, and another leader of the reform movement in the town, serving as mayor in 1847 and 1851. His son published Thompson's *History of Boston* in 1856.

141 The reform of the poor law in the 1830s led to the amalgamation of parishes and the erection of huge Union Workhouses, including this one in Skirbeck Road, Boston. It was designed by George Gilbert Scott (1811-78), as were others at Spilsby, Horncastle and Louth. In 1838 Scott married Caroline Oldrid, the daughter of the Boston draper.

142 This *Illustrated London News* picture of 28 October 1848 shows the first temporary railway bridge north of the Grand Sluice. The first railways in Boston opened in 1848 ran to Lincoln, Grimsby and Peterborough. The Great Northern Railway made Boston the headquarters of its lines in Lincolnshire and by 1900 the company was the largest employer in the town.

143 This shows the office of the Great Northern Railway's locomotive department which was in Boston from 1848 to 1852-3 when it moved to Doncaster, taking several hundred jobs with it. This site was the GNR locomotive depot for south Lincolnshire until 1964 and the offices and a small part of the site continued in use by British Railways until the 1980s.

144 The Great Northern Railway ended Boston's Georgian prosperity as the company took over the traffic in agricultural produce for London and elsewhere. This large railway granary built next to the Redstone Gowt Drain took the grain directly from vessels through its end doors. The granary burnt down in the 1980s, and Spalding Road now passes in front.

145 This view of 1986 shows the GNR passenger station built in 1850 to replace the initial temporary buildings. In 1911 a new booking hall was opened at the south end of this building, off the picture to the left, but then in 1992-3 the entrance shown here was splendidly restored as the main entrance, with a five-bay porch.

146 This view of *c*.1912 looks south over the extensive sidings of the goods yard from the Locomotive Street footbridge. A branch to the Park sidings curves left and the line to Grantham and Nottingham (opened in 1859) curves right. The GNR sacking store in the distance now has a non-railway use. Nowadays only the Grantham line remains.

147 The GNR civil engineer for south Lincolnshire was based in Boston. After his original premises in Stells Lane were burnt down on 12 August 1886, this new site was developed in Sleaford Road and the offices (*right*) and workshops (*left*) were occupied in 1894; in 1912 about 400 men worked here in connection with the company's premises and permanent way.

148 Boston-born Herbert Ingram (1811-60) became wealthy from the *Illustrated London News* which he founded in 1842. He was MP for Boston from 1856 until he drowned in Lake Michigan, after which this memorial statue was erected in St Botolph's churchyard, overlooking the Market Place. Before and during his time in Parliament Boston got very generous coverage in the *Illustrated London News*.

149 For seventy or so years after the arrival of the Great Northern Railway, the company steadily expanded its works in Boston and several streets of workers houses were built by speculators next to the line west of Boston. This view shows Duke Street, one of the first after 1848, named after Sir James Duke, MP, who was an active railway director.

150 The first part of Queen Street was built in the 1820s and named by supporters of Queen Caroline, but the section shown here, looking west, was developed after 1848 and linked the Broadfield Lane area to the passenger station. The houses on the far side were demolished 1966-7 for road widening.

151 St James' church in George Street was built as a chapel-of-ease to St Botolph's in 1861-4 to serve the needs of the railway community in western Boston. In Georgian times Anglicans had only built one small exclusive chapel and St James' was really their first belated response to the growth of the town. It was demolished in the 1970s.

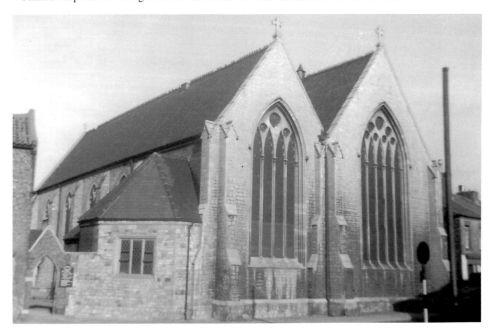

152 In the late 19th century Boston had four newspapers, in addition to the *Stamford Mercury*. Henry Farrow owned the *Boston Gazette* (published 1860-93) and in 1865 purchased the *Lincolnshire Herald* (published 1828-94); it was **not** founded in 1804! The *Boston Guardian* was published 1854-1958 and the *Boston Independent* 1879-1912 when it was replaced by the present *Lincolnshire Standard*.

The Lincolnshire Herald.

(ESTABLISHED 1804.)

THIS OLD-ESTABLISHED NEWSPAPER is the recognised Organ of the great Landed Proprietors and Farmers. There is no other paper, worthy of notice, published in the early part of the week, within 30 miles.

Price ONE PENNY.

FIRST EDITION PUBLISHED ON MONDAY EVENING. SECOND EDITION ON TUESDAY MORNING.

Offices :—MARKET PLACE, BOSTON.

The Boston Gazette.

FIRST EDITION PUBLISHED EVERY FRIDAY EVENING. Is the most popular Journal in this part of Lincolnshire, and is now the *ONLY* PENNY Newspaper in Boston circulating on SATURDAYS.

The *GAZETTE* is printed with powerful Modern Steam Machinery, and is taken by nearly all the leading Solicitors, large Firms, and Agriculturists in this part of the County.

THE GAZETTE CIRCULATES EXTENSIVELY THROUGH THE FOLLOWING TOWNS & VILLAGES :—

ALFORD	GAINSBOROUGH	NOTTINGHAM	STICKNEY
ALGARKIRK	GREAT GRIMSBY	PETERBOROUGH	SUTTERTON
BOSTON	HOGSTHORPE	SLEAFORD	SWINESHEAD
BRIGG	KIRTON	SIBSEY	TATTERSHALL
BUTTERWICK	LEAKE	SKIRBECK and	TRUSTHORPE
CONINGSBY	LEVERTON	SKIRBECK QUARTER	WAINFLEET
FRAMPTON	LINCOLN	SPALDING	WYBERTON
FREISTON	LOUTH	SPILSBY	WRANGLE
FRISKNEY	MARKET RASEN	STAMFORD	

OFFICES :—MARKET PLACE, BOSTON.   HY. FARROW, PROPRIETOR.

153 The *Lincolnshire Standard* became the main paper in the county, absorbing the *Boston Guardian* and the *Lincolnshire Chronicle* (of Lincoln) among others. It continued to be printed in Wide Bargate until the late 1980s and this picture shows the traditional scene of people queuing on a Thursday evening in 1986 to buy copies hot off the presses.

154 This view from the Grand Sluice railway bridge shows that the Boston Regatta on 2 August 1888 attracted huge crowds. The vessels on the Witham include long canal boats, larger Humber keels or sloops, and also an unidentified steamer. Notice the new trees on the left bank, which a century later still survive. (*See* no.52.)

155 No.30 Market Place (shown in 1910) was the post office from 1854 until 1885 and then Dr. Belton's surgery and the office of Sutcliffe & Co, shipping agents. In the 1950s the Trustee Savings Bank, which had been at no.31 since 1850, added no.30; it moved to Wide Bargate in 1967 and nos.30/31 were occupied by Royal Insurance until *c*.1990.

156 In the 1870s an old building in South Street (*see* no.20) was rebuilt as the entrance to the new brick Shodfriars Hall beyond. The architects were two sons of Sir G.G. Scott. Described as a Conservative Club in this 1873 drawing, it was opened in 1874 as a non-political social club and from 1877 the Conservative Association rented some offices here.

157 It is not known if Shodfriars Hall ever had the elaborate wall paintings shown in this architect's drawing of 1873. At the east end, not shown, was a stage where Arthur Towle (Lucan) first appeared in 1899 before achieving fame as Old Mother Riley. It closed as a theatre in 1929 but is still a social club.

158 Skirbeck Quarter Oil Mills (built 1870, and demolished in 1984) replaced an old windmill beside the Black Sluice (*left*). The smaller buildings are, left to right: 1870 mill house, old mill house/beer house *Three Jolly Lads*, toll-house for boats navigating the South Forty Foot Drain (beyond Black Sluice) and (partly hidden) turnpike toll-house for users of London Road until 1877.

159 In 1871 Boston Corporation created a 33-acre People's Park at South End, with flower beds, secluded walks, and open spaces for cricket and other games. They later gave an adjacent site where Boston hospital (shown here) was built; it opened in 1874 and developed until Pilgrim hospital opened in the 1970s. The dock took over the park in the 1930s.

160 This view shows the Corporation Swimming Baths in South End, opened 3 May 1880 and closed c.1965. They were designed by W.H. Wheeler and were on the site of the old shipbuilding 'docks'. This building replaced the old baths which the Corporation took over from a company in 1864. Here the old Bath Gardens (*right*) joined the People's Park (*left*) of 1871.

161 The opening of the Dock in December 1884 revived the port which has continued to grow and flourish ever since, taking over much land around it and beside the river for timber storage and other purposes. This early view, looking east, shows on the far side the entrance lock, dock office and fish landing building.

162 Close to the Dock entrance from St Johns Road is this range of workshops including the hydraulic engine house and tower (on the left) which operated the lock gates and other dock equipment. On the far right was the original house and office of the Corporation's Dock manager.

163 The traffic of Boston Dock included the export of coal and it had two coal hoists to raise railway wagons and tip their contents down chutes into the holds of ships. This one was erected in 1930 and demolished about 40 years later.

164 The character of Skirbeck Road has been radically changed by the development of the Dock since this picture was taken. In the distance on the right are gateposts and rails of the Union Workhouse. The field (*right*) is now a timber yard and so was the site of Hussey House (*left*) until *c.*1990, when Boston College acquired it for development.

165 The opening of the railway passenger station transformed West Street into a main shopping street of Boston, as is reflected in the exuberance of Day's Cash Stores. Apparently built in the 1880s for Arthur Forinton, house furnisher, it was Day's from *c.*1900 to 1964 (when it became a Wimpy Bar) and was demolished in the early 1980s.

166 Until 1896 churches and charities supplied all Boston and Skirbeck's public schools but then so many buildings needed replacing that School Boards had to be established. The Boston Board quickly built Park and Staniland schools, which lasted about ninety years, and this picture shows teachers and pupils at the Park Board Infant School in Tunnard Street in 1899.

167 This view shows the Staniland Board School, named after the Clerk to the Board. It was in Fydell Crescent and served the west side of Boston as Park School served the east, both schools following a very similar design. A separate board for Skirbeck built a school in Tower Road. All three schools have been demolished in recent years.

168 The Municipal Buildings in West Street were erected 1902-4 and initially housed nearly all departments of the Corporation, including the library, borough police station and fire station (shown here) as well as the school of art, town clerk, treasurer and other offices and the council chamber and committee room.

169 The post office in Wide Bargate opened by the Postmaster-General on 12 December 1907 had a public office, sorting office, and telephone and telegraph offices. It was extended towards the Central Park in 1935, but the sorting office moved out to Main Ridge in 1967 and the telephone exchange in 1970.

170 Rennie's bridge, after a century of use, had suffered so much from vessels running into it that it had to be replaced. This shows the demolition of the old bridge, with *Privateer* in front, in April 1913. In the background is the temporary footbridge, whose east end went straight into the Assembly Rooms. (*See* no. 46.)

171 The first sections of the new bridge designed by John W. Webster were soon lowered into place; it was built quickly and opened for traffic on 18 July 1913.

Bibliography

Bagley, G., *Floreat Bostona* (1985)

Bagley, G., *Boston—Its Story and People* (1986)

Bailey, I., *Pishey Thompson Man of Two Worlds* (1991)

Garner, A.A., *The Fydells of Boston* (1987)

Hackford, R.E., *Boston in Camera* (1990)

Lincolnshire Heritage, *A Guide to Life in Medieval Boston* (1994)

O'Neill, G., *Boston in old picture postcards* (1993)

Ormrod, W.M., *The Guilds in Boston* (1993)

Pevsner, N. and Harris, J., *The Buildings of England—Lincolnshire*, 2nd edn. revised by Antram, N., (1989)

Pomeroy, P., *Boston in Times Past* (n.d.; *c.*1990)

Thompson, P., *The History and Antiquities of Boston* (1855)

Wright, Neil R., 'Lincolnshire Towns and Industry 1700-1914' (1982), *History of Lincolnshire* Vol.11

Wright, Neil R., *The Book of Boston* (1986)

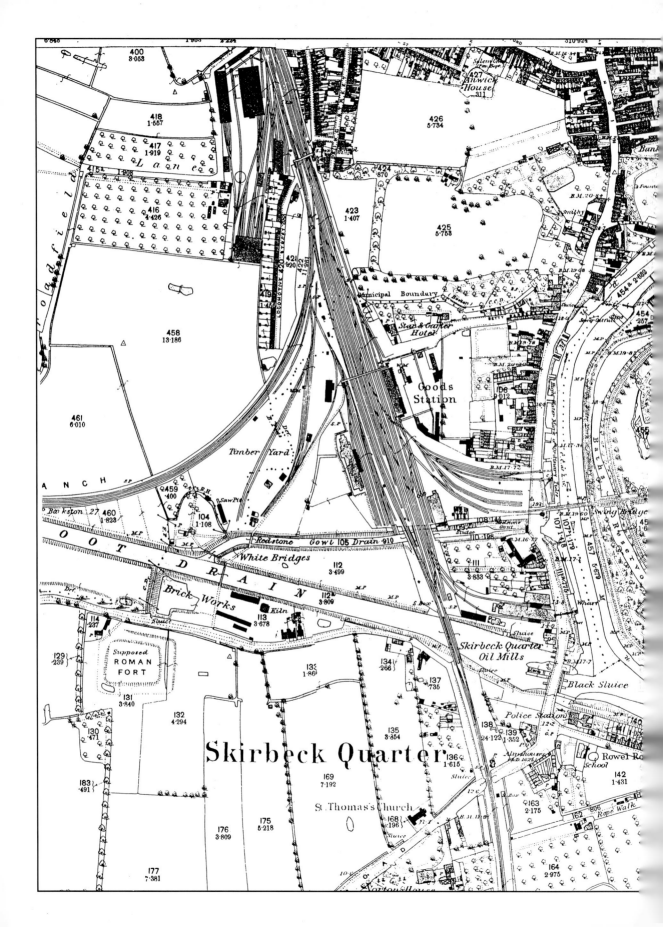